PRISONER TO POET

Thoughts Of An Incarcerated Soul

Devin D. Coleman

authorHOUSE®

AuthorHouse™
1663 Liberty Drive
Bloomington, IN 47403
www.authorhouse.com
Phone: 1-800-839-8640

First published by AuthorHouse   3/10/2010

ISBN: 978-1-4490-8229-1 (e)
ISBN: 978-1-4490-8228-4 (sc)
ISBN: 978-1-4490-8227-7 (hc)

Library of Congress Control Number: 2010901346

Printed in the United States of America
Bloomington, Indiana

This book is printed on acid-free paper.

DEDICATION

To my Grandma Rosalyn T. Coleman

I remember what you told me that day. I'm sorry for not being there
for you. I'm on my way though and I carry you in my heart.

I STILL BE LOVING YOU REAL HARD

ACKNOWLEDGEMENTS

I want to thank God for his grace and mercy. Thank you for removing and inserting people into my life at your discretion.

I want to thank my mom for all the sacrifices that she made on behalf of me. Thank you for your unwavering support and commitment to me.

To my step dad thanks for showing me what sacrifice is otherwise my poems would still be gathering dust. It's amazing how age, maturity, and responsibility can shed light on a situation.

To my dad Marvin Bell thanks for the letters and the money while I was away. We have certainly grown closer over the years and for that I won't complain. I know at times I was hard on you but I was a kid lost filled with so many questions and so little answers.

To my Baby Cuz Contessa Jones thank you for being you. Words can't express what you mean to me. Hopefully you have an idea. Thanks for not allowing me to be hard on myself.

Lisa those cards made the difference trust me! Charmaine (Bunny) thanks for not complaining about your phone bill!

My family I love you all. Forgive me for my disappearing acts. The kids DJ, Derrick, Donecia, Khaleel, Zaria, Deja. If you all don't know you all made the difference in my life! GG, Kesie Ma, Don Don, Aliera, Lil Alex, KeKe, Darien, Deja, Deshaun, Breezy, Chunk Man, Mari, Shanta, T man And Bree Bree I love you.

To my partners that rode the wave with me in no particular order. Mike (Deezie), Willie (Fat Boi), J, Eddie B, Mike Hut, T Dirt, Luke, Ced, Keith, Lil Gerald and family, Big Buh Dan, Mobb Boss and Frank Coleone (Hustle House), Shog, Telfair, Andre Sapp, Ellis, Hot Rod, Rob, Shawty Raw, Fatonya, Makisha, Loretta, Neidre, Khadeeja,

Twyler, Sharon, Keisha, Auntie Brandy, Mike Simms, Big Cuz Maurice, Chos (P.B.E.), Monkey E and those chess board matches as well as a host of other people that it would take all day to name.

Thanks to my comrades still behind that fence. Especially the ones that I kept up all night reading my poetry. Chaney aka Latif, Kojac, Bart Labistille aka ZO, Nip, Cali, Keith, Unk Scotty, D.A., Bugg, Maulsky, K-9, Big B, Willy Bo, Rolack, Stacy, Norman aka Bullet head, D. Brown, Charles Riley, JT, Ben, Tripplet, Trouble, and free my homeboy Donny aka west side finest!

If I left you out this time I will certainly catch you in the next one. Thanks to everyone who left an impression on my life.

Finally to the Author House staff thank you for helping to turn my dream into a reality.

FORWARD

Before you read this book you must understand that I wrote these poems when I was lost, confused, and in a great deal of pain. I was separated from life as I know it and then stripped of my identity, dignity, and self pride. I am not proud of everything that I have done but I regret nothing. The trying times as well as the bad decisions are as much of my make up as the triumphs and progress.

As you read these poems take them for what they are worth. At times they are my thoughts, my feelings, and at times a cry for help. Now I take full responsibility for my actions knowing that I define myself not the expectations of others no matter how good or bad. Sit back and enjoy the journey thru the Thoughts of an Incarcerated Soul.

CONTENTS

SECTION I

All the poems in this book reflect something that I've experienced or saw. Going from the "Free World" to living behind the fence is culture shock to say the least. It makes you think about things that were once apart of your life that may be no more. At times it causes you to turn the mirror on yourself. This particular section deals with how I felt about myself, the way I perceived the treatment from others, and how that created a shift in my mentality. At this time in my life I was separated from my family and my loved ones. I was stripped of my rights and my dignity. I was a broken man lost trying to find himself. Right or wrong these were my thoughts. All I ask is that you don't judge me until you walk a mile in my shoes.

A MILE IN MY SHOES

What you don't know can't hurt you?
That's a bunch of s**t!
Had I known what my mistakes
Would cost me,
I wouldn't be in this predicament.

It began before I could pin point it.
Came to light after I took my plea.
One that I considered family
Was my worst enemy.

Circumstances and situations
Play over and over in
My head.

As I lay in this prison bed
Wearing prison blues I'm
Grateful that I finally realized
That
I've been mislead.

Lead your own life!
Make your own decisions!
You have to live with them!

Besides...fulfilling costs to much.
All of this played in my head
And I still listened.

Not just about one thing, but everything.
That's what happens when your
Biological father isn't there.

You're left longing for a relationship
With a man. So you attach yourself
To the first one that acts like he cares.

Some youngsters are scooped up
By pimps, gangsters, drug dealers,
Molesters, even abusers.

My fate was to lie in the garden
With a snake slithering on his
Belly poisoning me with the venom of
False affection. As I looked deeper
In his eyes I saw the eyes of my accuser.

Hindsight is 20/20 and mistakes
Affect lives forever. I took advice
On my child, my case, and my
Relationship.

As I take off my prison blues when
The lights go out I realize that I
Can only blame myself.

Young, black, and angry. Angry
at the world because of the way
It looks at me.

Hopeless,
Useless,
A menace to society.

Truth be told I'm cold and alone!
Hungry for the love and acceptance
That always evades me.

That's why I act out at times.
That's how I get attention.
Otherwise no one knows
That I exist.

A grape that life sucked the energy
Out of forming a raisin that was
Aged thru trials and tribulations
Into a fine wine. That is used
To drown emotions that arises
When one takes time to reminiscence.

Before you envy a man because of the
Shoes on his feet realize that theirs
A price to pay. So before you purchase
Theirs ask yourself a question

Can I walk a Mile in
Their Shoes?

REMEMBER ME?

I'm him
The same person you use
To love and care about.
The one with the dreams
And ambitions.

Remember Me?

I had all the potential in the
World to.....
Be a graduate, a lover, a father,
A business owner...
Whatever I put my mind to.

Remember Me?

I'm the one who you used to call
When things were going wrong
And you needed a shoulder to
Lean on, to cry on, to shield you
From the pressures of the world.

Remember Me?

Then the day came when I
Made a mistake. When tragedy
Touched my life and I came to
You in my time of need.

You said you didn't
Remember.
You said you
Forgot....

Remember Me!

FAMILY

If you had family like me
Would you need enemies?
The one I felt were closet
Turned their backs on me.

Of course there were plenty smiles in my face
Along with many knives in my back.
By the time I began to realize it
I was in the middle of an all out attack.

My character was under assassination
And there was little that I could do.
If you were outside looking in
Would you believe their words were true?

My intentions were always to do right
Even still I've done some wrong.
Is that a reason to count me out?
Or was that the mission all along.

REFLECTIONS

Looking at my past
Has left me utterly confused.
Wondering what happened in my life
To make me fill these shoes.

Mom did the best she could
But I don't remember daddy there.
Well, only if you count the good times.
The bad ones caused him to disappear.

What did I do wrong?
To make him walk away?
No one to take me fishing
Or coach me on a date.

As a man I look in the mirror
At my face I cast a stare.
Am I looking at the shadow of a man?
If I am, who besides me cares?

Me and My Dad Reconnecting

I'VE BEEN (YET I BELIEVE)

I've been dejected,
Suffered thru rejection,
I've been ostracized
And also cast out.

I've been repressed,
Endured oppressive conditions,
And suffered thru depression
For quite some time.

Yet I stand before you steadfast
And unwavering, focused and
Relentless.

Something in my soul screams
"I can make it!"
"Dreams do come true!"

So even though I've been
Beat down, bruised,
And wounded I'm not going to
Stop and nurse my injuries.

I'll crawl until I can walk.
I'll plan and strategize until
Opportunity presents itself.

Unlike most I hear what people say…
I just take it as a grain of salt.
I believe I can make it,
Period!

I OFFER NO EXCUSES

Many mistakes made in a past
Often reminisced about.
A past filled with I should've done this,
I could've done that, and
Only if this hadn't happened.

Living in a world that doesn't
Accept excuses so why should
I offer any?

So I stand unapologetically
On my own two feet.
Eyes ablaze with concentration,
While my heart pumps ferociously,
As my focus and determination
Guides me to another plateau.

Not looking to the left nor the right
Because I don't judge myself with
What is around me. My compass lies
Within. I'm my own best friend
And my own worst enemy.

Winners are to busy getting back
From setbacks to come up with
Excuses.

Mistakes, failures, and disappointment
Are mere hurdles turned into stepping
Stones.

I jump over them, run thru them,
Or tear them down. Careful to
Pay attention to the lessons learned.

Victory is the main goal keeping in
Mind that if failure builds
Character, success unmasks it.

How can you appreciate a win without
Ever enduring a loss? How can you
Lead another when you're still trying
To find yourself?

How can you say I Love You, to another
And you have a hard time looking
Yourself in the mirror?

You Can't! So man up! And
Offer no excuses.

Me Solo

STRUGGLING TO LOVE MYSELF

As I look at myself
In the mirror naked…

I see the "proud flesh" protruding
From my chest. Scars on my
Knuckles show that I can
Hold my own.

But what does that prove?

Hair, eyes, ears, nose, mouth,
Arms and legs.
Is there more to me than
That?

Trying to look into cloudy
Eyes that know the truth
About what my flesh
Hides.

The fear of rejection
And failure. Jealousy
That reveals the feelings
Of inadequacy. Rage, anger,
And contempt for a society
That punished me for my
Weaknesses.

Deeper still is willingness
To overcome my shortcomings.

Ambition, loyalty and love!
Mixed with courage and strength.

Now I'm aroused by the thought
Of facing the unknown. Tired
Of waiting and ready to pursue
But first I must conquer myself.

So I can hold my head high and
Look unblinkingly into the mirror
Naked and unashamed.

REAR VIEW MIRROR

Sitting at a stop light while
Waiting for the light to change
I look into my rearview mirror.

First I was just looking at my face.
How it has matured over time. The
Childhood innocence it once held
Is long gone.

Smiles replaced by the scars of a
Painful past. Tear ducts clogged
Up and rendered useless.

As I look again into that same
Mirror and study my surroundings,
A habit learned from watching
People get shot up, jacked, and
Followed to where they lay their
Head just to get robbed. I
Notice that the light is green.

Everything is clear so I hit
The gas pedal and look at
The passenger side of my ride.

Its empty now, but it used to
Stay occupied. As a result of
Shady dealings, being crossed
And back stabbed I chose
To ride solo.

I figure it's the nest way to roll.
That way niggaz can't size me and
Women can't play up under me.

As I ride I make sure that
I don't see too many familiar faces
In the shadows or a car following
To close.

At times looking into that mirror
Is like looking into the reflection
Of a past that seems so far away.
Penitentiary chances, dead friends, and
Murdered foes. Mistakes made and
Scars to show the lessons learned.

But I did what I had to do to make
It. I was tired of being broke. Tired
Of dreaming about a big home and
Trips around the world. Does
The end justify the means?

Either way my main objective is
Keeping my head on my shoulders.
So from now on I'll continue
Looking into my rear view.

Big Bruh Dan and Mobb Boss of Hustle House

SOLITUDE'S STARE

Once a fulfilled man
Now is facing solitude's stare.
Love once resided in his heart
Now its only misery and despair.
So much has changed
In such a little amount of time.
Not noticing the changes occurring
Blinded by the sands of time.
Love no longer shown
As if it was a wasted emotion.
Hate crept in and took over
With no force or commotion.
Tried to be compassionate
Tried to live a normal life.
Then one incident happened
Leaving the residue of pain and strife.
Never forgetting what happened
Yet and still trying to move on.
Always aimed to do right
And ended up doing wrong.
Some say forgiveness is the key
But there isn't a hole in the lock.
As if it was filled with concrete
Now solid as a rock.
Tell me this…
Why should I forgive…and should I forget?
My whole life was altered
And I need to vent.
Can you hear me cry?
Better yet can you see my tears?
Living with a hole in my soul
Is one of my greatest fears.
What is my destiny?
What does the future hold?

Heard that it gets better
That's often what I'm told.
Looking toward the horizon
While trying to bend this corner.
Because of the trials I've been thru
I've decided to be a loner.

WHEN NO ONE CARES

Confined to the torment
That missed opportunities bring.
The what if's, I should have's
And only if freedom would ring.

I've endured the coldest winter in my life,
Looked myself in the eyes and saw the
Coldness that emits from a hollow heart.

Only because it seems that the things
I love the most are lost.
Everything I touch is corrupted
And everything I ask for is denied.

How can I love, trust, honor,
And commit?
The ones who supposedly loved me
Left me to die!

How can I take a man at
His words when most of
The men's words I hear
Are hollow?

I've healed but only awkwardly.
The scars are ugly and fierce.
They reach deep into my soul
And if you touch them I feel the pain.

When the wound breaks
And blood gushes forth
There are those that say
"You should forgive!"

I have forgave! I just can't
Afford to care anymore. I have
No desire to repair old
Relationships with those who
Saw me fall and didn't
Offer a hand.

That can only mean one thing
The relationship wasn't pure.
Wasn't sincere.

Now that I am able to walk and
Talk its okay to come around
Again?

But when I was battered and
Bruised it was unpopular to
Be around me.

At my lowest,
At my darkest,
At my most desperate moment,

NO ONE CARED!

SUICIDAL THOUGHTS

In a delusional state
Suicidal thoughts
Run rampant in my brain.
Wondering if my situation
Warrants it or am I
Going insane.
Started after a wound
Was inflicted, infected
And wouldn't heal.
Not physically but emotionally
Numb to the world
Wondering if anything is real.
Friendships based on convenience
And family trying to clean their face.
But in the depths of my soul
I'm alone missing without
A trace.
Should I go on or
Should I end it all here?
If I was gone forever
Would anyone shed a tear?
Have I fulfilled any capacity
To cause one to miss me?
Or was my life in vain
In that lies the mystery.
One part says "Move on,
Continue to press ahead!"
Then situations whisper in your ear
"What's the use, your better off dead?"
Like a wounded animal
My mind is succumbing to the pain.
Then I'm told that in the greatest losses
Is where you'll find the most satisfying gains?
The blind leading the blind

Leaving them lost in a secluded space.
Drained of all energy, yet trying to finish the race.
It's a difficult journey
When your loved ones forget
Your name.
Things may get better
But they'll never
Be the same.
I don't think I'll give
In. Not going out
Without a fight.
Victory is eminent
But after the pain
Of battle will I
Recognize its sight?

ALONE IN THE DARK

On the darkest night in
The darkest corner of the earth
In a darkened room with the
Shades pulled, a man sat alone.

Surrounded by four bare walls
He sat in the middle of the
Room deep in thought.

In front of him sat a mirror and
He peered deeply into it.
Not only because darkness
Surrounded him, but because
He tried to look into his soul.

He gazed into his own eyes, a
Pair he had seen on numerous
Occasions. He saw something
He had never seen before. Yet,
It looked familiar.

A tear fell, one after another,
Then he cried. A gut wrenching
Cry that cleansed his soul, not
A superficial cry used to draw
Sympathy and attention.

Staring back at him were the
Eyes that belonged to cold heart.
Frozen by mistakes made, consequences
Rendered and circumstances of his
Environment.

He thought about the warmer days
When he could sleep, when he
Could dream, when he could
Enjoy time with friends and family.

All of these times occurred before
Survival became priority number one!
Jealousy produced hatred and together
Hey walked hand in hand contaminating,
Festering, and destroying everything that
They came in contact with.

It was at that moment that his heart began to
Freeze over, without feelings or
Emotions maybe he could escape
The death and destruction that
Hatred and jealousy produced.

Little did he know that by allowing
His heart to turn could he would
Be alienating the very ones he
Wanted to save…his loved ones.

Tried as he did to reconstruct bridges
That were mangled by the cold winter that
His heart produced. Against his better
Judgment he tried to warm up, he
Tried to love again.

It was a feeling that overwhelmed him
And he couldn't describe it with the
Clarity it deserved, so he just basked
In it's presence.

As he opened the door to his heart
Wider and wider day-by-day envy
Saw opportunity to creep in.
Supported by hatred and resentment,
They crept in careful not to alert
Him to their presence.

And at his most vulnerable moment
They made themselves known.
Mounting and attack that was
Hard to fight alone. So
The love he once embraced
Receded into the depths of
His soul.

Now he sat in this dark room
Because he mourned for the love
That was now trapped in the
Darkness of his soul. Red flowing
Blood was now blue and frozen solid.

As he pondered this while looking into
His eyes at the past and present
Wondering what the future would
Bring he wept. Not caring to wipe
The tears that welled up in his eyes
And streamed down his face because
He was secure in his manhood.

The only thing that bothered him and
Now presented itself as his worst
Fear was…would he forever
Be a man alone in the dark.

HOLLOW EYES

Watching me stand here now
And seeing how I deal with
People.

The distance, the mistrust,
You'd think I've been
Like this for years.

I haven't though I used to feel.
I used to have emotions but
One moment in time changed
all that.

The burden of those feelings
Proved to be too much for me
To bear and I cut them loose.

It was either that or allow anger
And resentment to take hold
And eat me alive...Inside out.

That's why when you look at
My eyes they look hollow.
But if you take a deeper look,
Real deep...

You'll see what was once a loyal soldier.
One who believed and stood firm
On his word.

You'll see the pleasure of my
Life but it was stripped form
Me and pain set in.

You'll see my past because
That's the only thing that's clear.
You see my future is uncertain.

I'm a battered and bruised
Warrior in a land where
Soldiers are scorn because
They aren't beautiful
Anymore.

Their hands are calloused from
Handling things most men can't
Handle. Their skin is leathery
From weathering storms that
Most would evacuate from.

If I didn't discard my feelings
I wouldn't have survived.
It has been hard. I've seen
The strongest buckle!
The hardest cry!
And all the survivors
Have hollow eyes!

A SECLUDED PLACE

Hard times affect everybody
On this side of eternity.

It's at those times when you
Have to go to that special
Place to be alone.

It's a place where the clothes
That you're wearing don't matter.
Neither does the type of shoes on your feet.
The way your hair is cut, the way
Your body is built is irrelevant.

In that place your income,
Background or race doesn't
Even come into play.

That's the place you need to find when
The pressure of life is so hard that
It feels like four walls caving in
When nobody listens or cares. When
The weight of the world rests on
Your shoulders and you can't get
Any release.

Find that place to get your release.
Rejuvenate yourself. Sometimes we
Have to escape the immediate pressures
Of our reality in order to fortify ourselves
For the long haul.

So when life goes from raining to
Pouring, from better to worse, and richer
To poorer. You need to find your
Secluded place.

FIGHTING FOR MY LIFE

Been thru more trials and tribulations
Than a lifetime should allow.
Not only trying to be somebody
But trying to see another day.

Started off as a youngster fighting
Complications at birth.
From tumors to opening my
Eyes to observe this beautiful
Earth and its inhabitants.

Not knowing it then, but every time
My heart had a chance to beat
Warrior blood was pumped
Thru my veins.

It's a reason God put me here
And it seems like everyone and
Everything is trying to stop
My mission.

Make it known that I'm equipped
And plan, on fighting for my life
To the day of my demise.

I've been run over on multiple occasions.
I've even ran into a couple things
And each time I walked away.
Blood spilled and pain inflicted
But I still got up because I
Didn't know any better.

Gunshots blazing
Bullets being thrown and caught
Yet none came nigh my
Dwelling. Loved ones
And enemies are no longer
Here, casualties of war
Yet, I'm here keeping it
Moving towards my
Destiny.

Incarcerated in correctional
Institutions were the only
corrective behavior was
a foot up your butt by
a C.O. or a lock upside
your head by a
convict who felt slighted.

Destroying dreams and
Canceling plans.

Facing medical woes that
Would make the strongest
Mans knees buckle as
Mine did!

Then I thought about all
The things I've been
Thru. The things I avoided
And the God that kept
His protective arms
Around me. The one
Who said by my stripes
You are healed. The one
Who said No Weapon formed
Against me shall prosper.
No Fear is not an option
It's a commandment.

So, as I face the next trial
I lift my chin and stick
My chest out. I'm not
Untouchable, but I realize
That no weapon formed
Against me will prosper.

I'm fighting for my lie
And I plan on winning and
You can win too! God isn't
A respecter of persons
So when you're faced
With a trial or setback
Don't lay down fight.
Fight for your life!

SHELL OF A MAN

Tattooed tears don't fall they stain.
You were a loved one yet you left me in the rain.
There's no more love just hurt and pain,
Crossed by my family leaving a shell of a man.

A DIAMOND IN THE ROUGH

It started out as a
Hunk of coal in a
Mine buried hundreds
Of miles under the earth.

At first it was nothing special to look at.
But the circumstances surrounding
That hunk if coal is what
Makes it different.

Over years of tremendous pressure
Being piled on that piece of coal
It didn't break or become dust.

The protective covering that to some
Looks black and nasty begins
To peel away or dissolve to reveal
The beauty that lies beneath.

What it once was is no longer,
Now what you have is a diamond
Formed from the roughest of
Circumstances, which makes it
Marvelous to behold.

Its beauty sparkles in the sunlight
And is world-renowned.
People have lost their lives
Behind this beauty. Some even
Sell their soul.

What once was a mockery
Is now the sharpest and most
Beautiful stone around.

At times I liken myself
To the diamond in the rough.
Because I was that coal that
Everyone wanted buried.

Life took its course and tremendous
Pressure was applied. I lost loved
Ones to what I viewed as untimely
Deaths or just strained relationships.
Friends either died in the streets or
Turned out to be back stabbers.

My main lady couldn't be trusted and I
Found out after I lost one child to a
Miscarriage and another to another
Guy even though she claimed the
Baby was mine.

I started throwing bricks at the penitentiary
And one got stuck. Causing me to be separated
From everything and everyone that cared
About me and gave me hope.

Then during the dark recesses of that isolation
The ugliness of what my life had become began
to peel away.

My light started to shine.
In spite of being oppressed
And degraded at every turn.
My talent shown thru the darkness.

When my never give up attitude
Became more clear. And then
I began to stand apart from the crowd.

That's when the ones who turned
Away from me in the ugliness
Of my transgressions saw the
Beauty that now is emitted
From my pores.

Now in order to be apart of that
Beauty that has and will continue
To become my life will come with a price.

Swallowed pride, apologies, and
Requests for forgiveness. Some can
Afford the price but for many it
Will be too much to pay.

But whatever the cost you
Can never copy or cheapen
To the beauty emitted form
A Diamond In The Rough.

SECTION II

This section deals with the loss of my grandmother. That in itself was a blow. I mean she was my friend, my advisor, my buddy, and we could talk about just about everything. I was devastated when I found out that she passed away. I knew it though because when I called she didn't answer. Here I am sitting in the middle of nowhere because of a selfish mistake and my family needs me. Everybody deals with it but when you're so far away from your support system it makes it that much worse. I was at a crossroads but I had some troopers on my team in the form of my mother, sister, and a couple dedicated cousins (Contessa, Lisa, and Charmaine) that never gave me and opportunity to give up on myself thank you! I wrote some words to express my feelings towards you all.

ACTIONS

Actions speak volumes
Words are merely the echo!

MY GRANDMA

I should have listened
Now I'm in prison
Laying on my bunk
In the middle of the night
Thinking.

Wanting to go crazy
But trying to hold on,
I lost someone special today.

My Grandmother…

But she was more than that to me
She was my friend,
My confidant,
My advisor.

She didn't judge me,
She counseled me.
She took time to deposit
Jewels of wisdom inside me.

She was strong and wise
Her presence is so strong
That I feel it and miss
It at the same time.

It's two things she never did,
Fail or complain.

She experienced things in her day
That my generation would
buckle under.

She experienced things that we were
Told about…
Discrimination, Segregation, and Blatant Racism.

She grew up in the Civil Rights Era
And witnessed the decline of
The black family.

She saw what drugs did to our
Communities and she was there when
Fathers began leaving home.

My grandma was apart of the era when
Women carried themselves
With dignity.

They were strong, supportive, and proud
While being gentle, sweet, and uncompromising.

When men courted women they met the family
Before they saw the family jewels. No matter
how hard the day was when night fell
daddy was home.

She was around when our people had honor
And knew who they were to having no
Shame and trying to find themselves.

She never complained.
When worse came to worse
She stayed strong.
She may have shed
Silent tears but her
Chin was held high.

Failure was not an option.
How could I give her an
Excuse after all she'd
Been through?

What do I know about
Making food stretch
Or wondering were
The next meal was
Coming?

Only what she told me.
Another thing she always
Knew where her kids
Were and who
They were with.

My Grandma is my hero.
She invested in me when
The world told her
Contrary.

When rotten fruit fell form my tree
She didn't panic, she watered me with
Love and fertilized me with wisdom.

She left some pretty big shoes to fill.
Just maybe if I heed her directions
I can follow the path she left.

The path of wisdom, integrity,
Love, courage, strength, and
Honor.

Grandma,
I still be loving you!
REAL HARD!

One of my hardest stops

REMINISCING ABOUT MY GRANDMA

Waiting around lost looking for someone to look up to.
It wasn't until I lost my Grandma that I realized
How strong her presence was.

I'm talking about my sweet beautiful grandmother
Full of grace, strength, and integrity.
Wisdom poured out of her like water
From a faucet. It's within reach you just
Have to turn it on.

I remember the times she dropped jewels on my
Life and I had that yeah but mentality.
Now I'm beginning to realize who I was
Actually speaking to.

Sitting on my bunk praying that she makes it
But she doesn't. Looking at her face
Thru a memory that's burning bright.
The smile on her face captivates me as
Her fine hair blows in the wind.

She's the biggest cheerleader that I've known.
Rooting for me when the cards were
Stacked against me and people
Counted me out.

I SHOULD'VE BEEN THERE

I'm sitting here looking
At this picture realizing
That she won't be there
When I get home.

But I still have to hold
Up my side of the agreement.
So, for now I have to be strong.

It's nothing like receiving the phone call
That you pray never comes.
Your legs buckle, your eyes water
All while your mind goes to
Another place, another time.

Remembering days that can't be repeated.
Conversations that will never be held
And dreams that won't be realized
Together. And it hurts.

Being absent doesn't
Make it easier. What ifs
And what happened roll off
Your tongue but what
Really plagues your mind is
I should've been there!

Regardless as to what
This person or that person did.
Regardless of what this doctor said.

I still believe my voice would've made
The difference because hers made
The difference in my life when
Circumstances were on my neck,
Murder in my heart and
Rage in my blood.

I gotta get it together,
I gotta hold on,
I gotta make it,
I made a promise!

I Still Be Loving You!!!

CHEERING SECTION

I know you're used to me
Being in voice range when
The game is on the line.

In the last quarter, in the final minutes
When you normally look for my encouraging
Face and strain to hear my voice over
The crowd.

Now when you look around
You can't see me or heat
My voice because I'm so
Far away.

Rest assured that I'm still
With you. My seat is just
A little further away from
All the action.

All you have to do is picture
My face with my mouth wide
Open and put all the words
In it that you need to hear.

"You're going to make it!"
"Never give up!"
You know the things that
You told me when the
Weight of the world
Was on my shoulders.

And when that's not enough
Extend your hand, turn your
Palm up and close your eyes.
Then you'll feel the warmth
Of my touch.

I won't say that "I'll be there
For you" because I've never left.
I'm still in your cheering section
Supporting you from miles and
Miles away.

NO MORE

No more hatred
No more racism
No more discrimination

No more pain
No more sorrow
No more disappointments

No more letters
No more phone calls
No more visits
No more love packages

No more setbacks
No more let downs
No more waiting on someone who'll never show.

THINKING OF MY MOTHER

When I think of my mother
And all the trouble she has been thru
Trying to raise a baby boy
When the world told her to cut him loose.

She was nominated for the job
Even though my daddy wasn't ready yet.
She received no stellar awards
Neither has she ever voiced a regret.

She ushered me thru school and
Sent me to college too.
Then when I made a mistake
She road to the penitentiary too.

Visitation was always jubilant
My heart warmed by the sight of her face.
If she was disturbed or disappointed
She didn't show a trace.

When I think of my mother
I think of courage and strength.
Fear was not in her vocabulary
You couldn't see it or smell its scent.

She always told me to remain strong
And to my convictions stay true.
She told me to trust in God
Because he'd surely bring me thru.

When I think of my mother
I want to make her proud of me.
I want to achieve some great accomplishment
For all the world to see.

We've seen some tough times together
But somehow we have made it thru.
She said if I believed in God
He'd make all my dreams come true.

So to this warrior of a woman
I've dedicated the rest of my life.
When the circumstances said she was wrong
In her heart she knew she was right.

UNCONDITIONAL LOVE

In my darkest moment
When I needed someone
But felt like no one cared.

I looked around
And you were there.

In all your splendor
Regardless of what
Was going on in your life.

You decided
To stand by me.

Born as my cousin
You chose to become my friend
And decided to love me...
Unconditionally!

I've known no love as true
Or friendship as
Enduring as ours.

It has to be
God Given.

The sands of time have
Been tested and
You remained true.

Distance has been stretched
And you have remained a letter
Or phone call away.

Honesty, loyalty, and support
Have been given to me

By you.

Which is a true representation
Of the words you spoke
When you said…

Love Unconditional

No river is wide enough,
No ocean deep enough,
No desert dry enough,
To keep me at bay
When you call!

New meaning has been given
To the words…
I'll be there for you!

What words can't say
Actions will show…

Love

Your tears will roll down my cheeks,
Your disappointments cause me pain,
Your success takes me to another level of joy!

When doors appear to close in your face,
When hurdles get in your way,
When you approach walls that appear insurmountable,
We'll overcome them together!

Bonded by materials
That doesn't whither when heat is applied,
That doesn't burst when pressure is present,
That doesn't hide when situations are unpopular.

Love Unconditional

My smile, joy, and strength…Baby Cuz

THE HEART AND SOUL OF A WARRIOR

Every morning
When the day breaks
A warrior must be
Prepared to fight.

Not some days but everyday!

They are not all blessed
With the luxury of
Rest or free time.

From sunrise to sunset they fight.
When others are asleep they plan.
When everything is quiet they
Are ever vigilant.

Not wanting their opponent
To get the upper hand. Their
Very existence depends on
Minimizing mistakes made
And paying close attention
To detail.

When adversity does strike
Warriors don't panic.

They conjure up strength
From the depths of there
Soul and fight for what
They believe in…
Until Death!

Sometimes a warrior may
Be faced with a battle and
Everyone they ever knew or
Were kind to turns their back!

When an injury is inflicted
Some decided to walk away. A real
Warrior doesn't let that deter them
From reaching their objective, it's all
The more reason to!

They take a stand and
Refuse to give any ground,
Failure is not an option!

No retreat, No Surrender

SECTION III

This section here is for the young people that look at the videos and hear the music and want to jump in the streets head first. Yeah everybody wants to have nice things such as money, cars, and all the things that come along with it. Just know that with every action is a reaction. Nobody is untouchable. For everybody that lived thru it they can give you a list of friends that died in the streets, caught time and never came home. Many can tell you how they had to watch their kids grow up thru visits or talk to their family thru glass partitions. Can you hold your own then? Will you still be true to the game?

A SOLDIER'S LIFE

At the crack of dawn two men awaken.
Both are headed for war but on
Different battlefields.

One dresses in camouflage fatigues
With a Government Issue rifle over
His shoulder and a 45 at his side
Along with a helmet on his head.

The other dresses in blue jeans and a
Fresh white tee. Fitted cap on his
Head. Dog tags replaced by tattoos
2 Glock 9's by his side.

The first soldier defends his country
The second defends his block.
Neither one knows if today is
Their last day on earth.

Before they set out for the day
Their prayers are the same.
"Lord, watch over me and
allow me to return home safely.
Please don't let me freeze in the
Heat of battle or allow my gun to jam!"

One hops in a tank prepared to give
His life for the rights and privileges
Of others. While the other jumps in
A 500 Benz with 22 in run flat tires.

He's also prepared to give his life,
But it's for the love of the dough.

Both soldiers rely on wits and
Instincts. A clear head and solid
Team. No retreat, No Surrender.
Win or lose putting up a fight
And refusing to be taken alive.

Bloodshed on the battlefield leads
To tears shed and lost comrades.
No time for reflection because
A moment's hesitation could
Lead to a suit knocking on the
Front door of your next of kin.

In a war when one life is lost another
Recruit is ready to fill those shoes
And make a name for himself.

Both the war on a foreign land
And the war on the streets are
Argued and protested against.

But until the powers that be find
A solution keep a full clip and
Sober mind. Then maybe
You'll live long enough to
Tell the true story of a
Soldier's Life.

East Side Florida Avenue

SO YOU...

So you want to be a champion?
Are you willing to pay the price?
Getting up early in the morning
And staying out until the middle of the night.

So you want to be a hustler?
Are you willing to pay the cost to be the boss?
Are you willing to shoot to kill in a moments notice?
If not you've already lost.

So you want to be a fighter?
Do you have what it takes?
Are you willing to take a punch to give one?
All for the sake of winning.

So you want to be a leader?
Can you live with the decisions to be made?
Even if it means putting someone else's life at stake
And the possibility of sending them to the grave.

It doesn't matter so much
What you want to be.
As long as you're prepared to do
What you have to do.

Regardless of resentment and accusations
To your calling you must remain true.

Telfair on the Avenue

YOU MUST BE WILLING

In order to kill
You have to be
Willing to die.

In order to fight
You must be
Willing to lose.

In order to succeed
You must be
Willing to fail.

What are you willing to do?

In order to rise
You must be
Prepared to fall.

In order to speak
You must know
How to listen.

In order to walk
You must first
Begin to crawl.

What are you willing to do?

In order to appreciate the light
You must know what darkness is?

In order to recognize excess
You must first know lack.

In order to appreciate loyalty
You must know betrayal.

In order to bask in victory
You must know the
Agony of defeat.

What are you willing to do?

Whatever it takes!

TWIN 45'S

It's dark outside
And the night is surrounded
By an eerie silence.

I don't want to go out
But my hand has been forced.
Words have been exchanged
And I live and die by mine.

As I take the safety
Off my twin 45's
I pray they don't jam.

I'm dressed in all black
In hopes that my mom
Won't have to wear the same colors next week.

I heard that
If you live by the gun
You die by it.

It's funny how life is that way.
I stand before him in a black hat,
Black jeans, black shoes, toting
2 black 45's and he turns ghostly white.

The last thing he saw was
The muzzle fire from my pistol
And his last words were Damn!

GUN POWDER RESIDUE

I'm wearing gunpowder residue
And that dude lying on the ground
Is wearing my shells.

Two lives tossed away
Repping a life and a block
That they could never call their own.

One is doing life in prison
The other is doing life in hell.

Kids growing up fatherless
Because daddy's way of living
Caused him to live by the
Gun and keep an extra
Clip full of shells.

Bustin' at back-stabbers
And rumblin with the vultures.
Better to wear gunpowder residue
Than let six of your homeboys
Tote you.

UNTITLED

It's been a long time since
I've had my hand held
Or seen a friendly face.

Years of being crossed and
Back stabbed got me looking over
My shoulder moving at a snails pace.

Glocks by my side as a pre-caution
But I'd much rather use my brain.

I've just seen to much blood shed
Over the years of young men dying
Still screaming, "Long live the game!"

If money motivates jealousy and
Envy, then with these Glocks
I'll have to live.

In spite of what people may
Say or think I only have
One life to give.

DISTANCE YOURSELF

Every since this tragedy occurred in my life
I've been trying to make sense of it.
I could blame this person or that one
But is my analysis legitimate.

Storm clouds surround my life
And the rain pounds me all the daylong.
I find myself wondering if this will pass over
If so, how much longer do I need to be strong?

I've seen friends turn to foes
I've also seen family turn away.
So when the sun breaks thru the clouds
I must go my separate way.

I distance myself from negativity.
I distance myself from fear.
Once thought I had many loved ones
Now they choose to steer clear.

Eventually I must move away from this madness
Put an end to this horrible game.
Explore different opportunities
In a land where no one knows my name.

DOWN AND OUT

At the times when I was ballin'
You were my number one man.
Then times started looking bas
So you picked up your things and ran.

Honestly money isn't coming
In the same fashion that it did before.
All that came to a halt
When I parted those penitentiary doors.

I went from putting on custom-made gators
To wearing state issued bro's.
I had an assortment of clothes in my closet
Now my clothes are being chose.

Once received accolades and admiration
Now its just stares of disbelief.
Streets once had my back
All of that has now come to a cease.

That's what happens when you're down and out
No one remembers your name.
Hold your head lil soulja
Charge that lesson to the game.

BID YOUR TIME

There is a time and season
For everything under the sun.
You're concerned with the battle
But I'm fighting until the war is won.

Have you ever heard of the race
Between the tortoise and the hare?
Meaning, because I'm moving slowly now
Theirs no reason to despair.

I'm steadily moving ahead
Striving at my own pace.
Not to worried about the competition
Because slow and steady wins the race.

Run by me now
Only because I've had a setback.
But thru time, patience, and perseverance
I'll be sure to make my come back.

So, I'm looking down the path
Knowingly bidding my time.
As long as the sun continues to rise
I'll have my time to shine.

FLIP SIDE

Listening to these rappers
Got these jitterbugs confused.
Telling them about the shine
But leaving them ignorant to the rules.

Everybody screaming dope boy
Even our ladies want apart of the game.
Everybody don't get rich
They get robbed, do time, or get slain.

So you have a nice whip, big home
Even got some change.
But remember when your life is over
You leave the world how you came.

Lil mama screaming that she loves you!
Your homeboys say there gonna hold you down.
Get knocked off and go to the penitentiary
And you'll see who comes around.

Your time goes by, you're getting short
You even have a plan.
Then letters start coming. It's lil ma
Screaming she wants you to be here man.

Them niggas find out your coming home
They throw a party and blow some trees.
On the surface you act like its all good
But on the inside you say "Where were you in my time of need?"
This is the flip side of the game young playa
You better listen hard and begin to take heed.

THIS LIFE WE LEAD

Sitting on this plantation
Disguised as a prison.

Watching black males travel
In packs like animals in the jungle.

Life as we knew it begins to disappear.

No longer do we have the ability
To make certain decisions
Concerning our own well-being.

No longer do we have freedom
To choose meals, clothes, and
Living quarters.

The days of spending time with
Family and friends are long gone.

The days of kickin it with the
Fellas is history.

Dreams are replaced by
Nightmares of our reality.

Confidence is diminished
Day by day and hope is
The silver lining to the dark
Clouds hovering over us.

Friends disappear and family
Is all of a sudden too busy.

Letters begin to come less frequently
And phone calls are now answered
Sporadically.

All we have to hold on to are
Faded dreams and fantasies
Of a better tomorrow.

My Homeboy Donny

MY BROTHER'S KEEPER

In an ideal world where
People do no wrong
Then I am my brother's keeper.

But in the society that we
Live in now, he can't count
On me. I'm sure to let someone
Creep him.

Am I my brother's keeper?

Only time he'll get a smile
From my face is when I'm
Planting a knife in his back.

Otherwise I'll watch his moves
Waiting for him to slip and
I'll come at him in all black.

Am I my brother's keeper?

Yeah, I know the world is
Against us. That it's hard for
Us to get a job and he has
Three mouths to feed.

That's none of my concern. I
Can't let him get more than
Me because my heart is
Filled with greed.

I watched him go to school and
Work hard. All the while I called
Him green.

When I get off Work I'm dirty and
I get mad at him because when he
Leaves his place off work it seems that
He's always clean.

Am I my brother's keeper?

Yeah right, maybe another
Place and another time.

The only time he can count
On me is when I'm testifying
To help him get convicted of
A crime.

I watched him shackled and
Shipped to prison. Man, what
A life to lead.

He thought that I was his brother
Because we shared a color. Goes to
Show that he shouldn't have
Counted on me!

Am I my brother's keeper?

Yeah, until his family is involved.
Playing up on his woman. Telling
Her everything he's doing and
Everything he's already done.

He's so blinded by the idea of
Me watching his back. He doesn't
Even notice what I've done.

Am I my brother's keeper?

How can I be? I've been
Jealous of him since day
One. I know that I've
Had every opportunity
To have a family, wealth, and health.

But I want what belongs to him.
I've been so busy stalking his
Success that I let mine pass
Me by. So I have to play
The cards that I was dealt.

Am I my brother's keeper?

Yeah, I'm helping society
Keep its foot on his neck.

IT COMES WITH THE BID

I called home today
Trying to hear the voice of a loved one.
Today was a rough one,
To make matters worse my call was denied!

I had to remind myself,
It comes with the bid.

Sitting on my bunk
Watching the C.O. call the mail.
Looks like today isn't my day.
Come to think of it, yesterday wasn't either!

I wanted to click and go off but,
It comes with the bid!

Checking my canteen card.
I have to buy some hygiene.
My turn is next,
Awe man, it read $0.00!

It comes with the bid.

I seen dude get his head cracked.
Another guy got stabbed in retaliation.
Then found this dude screaming "Thug Life"
But he's kissing a boy at night.

I guess you know,
It comes with the bid.

You have lifers, repeat offenders,
Even first time offenders.
Just because you've been
Blessed with a date don't
Take it for granted.
If you cross the wrong
Dude at the right time
Going home won't

Come along with your bid!

TRYING TO CHANGE

Hard times
Bring harder choices.

Like…
Should I hit a lick
Or cop some blow.

Should I wait outside
Or just kick in his door.

I don't want to
Live like this
But what can I do.

Go to college…
Get a job…
Start a family…
Own a business…

It sounds good
But I get stuck on 1 question.

HAVE YOU EVER COMMITED A FELONY?

If it doesn't matter
Then why ask?

It limits my educational funding
It limits my job prospects and
Income potential.

It limits my ability to obtain a loan
For a home or business.

Which in turn prohibits me from
Effectively taking care of my family.

As a matter of fact
The only place I haven't seen that question
Is on a W-2!

I thought when I was released from
Prison my papers said…

TIME SERVED!

Some people say
"Don't use that as a crutch go
get a job. Do something for
yourself."

But when you find out about
My past…
You clutch your purse
You stare and whisper and
You stop frequenting my
Establishments!

I don't want a handout
I want a fair shot.

I don't want your pity
I want an opportunity to prove myself.
I don't want to take anymore
I want to give!

Me and E on the Chessboard

HOLD YOUR HEAD (DEDICATED TO ISAIAH CALDWELL AKA ZEKE)

Just because you're a soldier doesn't mean
That you have to be strong all the time!

It means regardless of the situation or circumstance
You have to hold your head.

Every man has fears and sheds tears.
Sometimes it comes to light in a public way.
Sometimes your hurt is displayed in a public way.

In those times know that "we" (your brothers thru the struggle)
Have your back, front, and both sides
110% of the time, 24 hours a day, and 7 days a week!

Dedicate your life to the one who loved you! In spite of!
And encouraged you to be the best that you could be.

STAY STRONG, 1 LOVE

SECTION IV

This section here is hard for me to classify. I was going thinking about some things and wrote down my thoughts. It was at a time when I had to motivate myself to keep on going. I figured if it helped me maybe there is one more person that can relate.

A SINGLE TEAR

A single tear drops…
For all the miscarriages,
The still borns and all
The babies born dependant
On drugs.

A single tear drops…
For the little girl who
Wants to be a woman and
The little boy who wants
To be a man but are confused
By their role models.

A single tear drops…
For all the single women
Left alone to raise children
Because their men duck
Out on their responsibility.

A single tear drops…
For all the woman that are
The victims of domestic violence,
And for the men who are arrested
Because their women use the system
As a means to control them.

A single tear drops…
For all the men that are incarcerated
And will never have an opportunity
To kiss, hug, or converse with
Loved ones again.

A single tear drops…
For all the felons that heard the
Words time served but still can't
Vote or get a job but have
To pay taxes.

A single tear drops…
For all those who are effected
By the criminal justice system. The
Offenders, the families, the friends, the kids,
And the neighborhoods that
Miss them.

A single tear drops…
For the victim of the stray bullet,
The dreams they'll never achieve,
The sights they'll never see, and
The lives they'll never be apart of.

A single tear drops…
For all the victims of cancer
And the family and friends that
Support them.

A single tear drops…
For all the victims of the HIV/AIDS
Epidemic that were unknowingly
Infected.

A single tear drops…
For all those hearts
That stay warm regardless
Of how cold the world
Treats them.

A single tear drops...
For those that stayed
Strong and held there
Dignity inspite of.

A single tear drops...
For those who achieve.
In spite of criticisms
And the no's that they've
Had to face.

A single tear drops...
For those that achieve success
And remembered the neighborhoods
That molded their minds and
The people that helped shape there
Personality.

A single tear drops...
For the struggle,
And all those trapped
In it.

VISIONS

Hidden in my thoughts
Clouded by doubt
But pushed thru by sheer determination
Lies the will to win.

Visions of better days
Are what carry me through the tough days.
The ones when money is short
And comrades die.

Poverty is nothing new,
Being crossed in the game
Is no new occurrence.

Yet, visions of better times
Propel me thru my todays
To usher me into my tomorrow.

DIE ANOTHER DAY

How close have you been to death?
To smell its stench.
To see rigor mortis set in.
To have the casket closed and lowered.
Dirt thrown on top.

Stagnation surrounds you.
Everyone is sad.
So many what ifs and I should haves.

Don't let your dreams die that death
Reach out to them.
Breathe life into them thru a plan.
Stare rejection in the face and scream
"I shall not be moved!"

Feed your soul so it will flourish.
Let life abound from within.
Pass thru the storm and let the sun
Shine on your future.

Refuse to let your dreams die!
Refuse to let your soul whither!
Refuse to let your heart become cold!
Die another die!

A VOICE

I am reluctant to move on
Yet to far ahead to turn back.
I must gird up my strength
And prepare for their attack.

My character has been deflated
My self-consciousness all but destroyed.
Through the spreading of propaganda
Which is the strategy they employ.

In order for survival I must unite
With those of a like mind.
But through years of ignorance
My neighborhood has been polluted with crime.

We need to become solidarity in action
Creating a wave of tremendous force.
Only then will we elevate our mentality
And become a people with a voice.

LOST

A disenfranchised people
Which is no coincidence
Slavery is years past yet its
Remnant still exists.

Bamboozled and befuddled
Under the pretense of equality.
Yet in day to day life
That remains to be seen.

Persecuted and perplexed
Trying to find our way.
We must get from under confusion and illusion
Then we will have our day.

ONE REVOLUTION

Dreamed by two different men,
Born into two different times,
Living two different lives,
Using two different methods
To reach two different crowds.

Having two different prison sentences,
Leading two different roles,
Which lead to two premature deaths
In pursuit of one goal.

Revolution

SECTION V

In this section I was having fun. I called myself trying to make a play on words. I'm primarily trying to draw parallels between life and natural occurrences. Nature is very powerful and so are a man's emotions.

THE VOYAGE

Two ships sail a long in the sea.
It's a pleasant enough day.

The wind is blowing.
The dolphins are jumping out of the water.
The birds are commanding the air.

I would have never appreciated the scenery
If your ship didn't pass me in that waterway.
At that particular time.

I owe my vision and determination
To you, the captain of that ship.

Even if we never pass one another again
Be assured that I am forever indebted to you.

HUNGER AND THIRST

At times I've been so hungry
That my stomach touched my back.
It was a pain so fierce that I couldn't bring myself to sleep.

I've been so thirsty
That I literally became cotton-mouthed
On the brink of dehydration.
At that moment water couldn't quench my thirst.

That's when I knew that I had to pursue my dreams.

I've recently found that success will
Quench my thirst, and clearing
Hurdles to accomplish a goal will fill my hunger.

So, when you see my face askew
Know that it's only a mask of
Determination needed to
Fill my stomach and quench my thirst.

TURBULENT WATERS

A sailboat is traveling in the sea on a sunny day.
Flocks of birds invade the airways,
As schools of fish migrate along the waterway.

The wind is blowing a gentle breeze
And there isn't a cloud in the sky,
Giving the aura of a peaceful tranquility.

Suddenly the sea begins to speak volumes
Sending waves crashing against the vessel
Demanding immediate attention.

The sailboat that once traveled
As one with the ocean
Is now being tossed to and fro
With reckless abandonment.

The inhabitants of this vessel
Have only two options at the moment.
Either relinquish themselves to the mercy
Of the sea, or forge ahead in spite
Of the obstacles in front of them.

At times life throws storms
Into our lives to rock us from
A state of complacency.

At those times we are forced
To analyze the situation and ourselves
And decide to either progress or regress.

Then and only then
After a reality check
Can we weather the storms
Of today into the sunny
Shores of tomorrow!

Downtown Jacksonville

BLUE

Blue represents many things. Its
Up to us how it reflects in
Our lives.

Blue is the color of my prison uniform.
It's confining and oppressing. It serves
As a reminder of the results associated
With a past that I'm desperately
Trying to escape.

Blue is the color of my song and the song
Of many others who used words and
Rhythm as a method to express sorrows.

Blue is the color of the ocean as it
Stretches to meet the sand on the
Beach. Flowing water to either
Bring you in or take you out depending
On your destination.

Blue is the color of the sky on the sunniest
Of days. The ultimate freedom where
Bird's fly and eagles soar. Defying
The pull of gravity that desperately
Tries to hold them down.

Blue is a powerful color. Even in
My prison uniform I can be
Sad, or I can ride the waves
Of the sea to the highest heights
Of my life and soar like an eagle!

Blue! What does it represent
For you?

STORMS

Everyone hits a point
In their lives when they
Find out who their
Real friends are.

The ones who were
There when you graduated,
Got married, got a raise, or
Signed that big contract.

The ones who smiled in
Your face when you made
That big play or cast the lead
In the new production.

Trouble comes and they fade
Away. Like the sun does when
Rain clouds appear.

When the car breaks down,
You lose your job, you get
Sick or you're not famous
Anymore.

When you get arrested
And catch time.

Everyone gossips about it
And you here the "I can't
Believe that" or the "I told you so"

No one mentions the good
Times when you baby-sat,
Loaned out money, or worked
On their car, all for nothing
In return.

That's when you know that the true meaning
Of friendship because real friends give
Until it hurts. They don't contradict you
In public. They stand by your side and
When you're wrong they tell you face to face
And still watch your back.

Even though no one likes or enjoys the
Storms of life. They are necessary to cut
The fat from your life so you can finish
Your journey.

SNAKE IN THE GRASS

It's a beautiful field
Filled with immaculate green grass,
Healthy trees, some swaying in the wind,
And of course an amazing watering hole.

Who would ever imagine
There was a snake lurking
In all that beauty.

Slithering on its belly
Going to and fro searching
For anyone or anything
To spoil. Simply because the
Snake can't accept its fate.

Remember misery
Loves company.

Therefore, when your life
Suddenly begins to resemble
A beautiful meadow with
A brook of flowing water.
Be ever vigilant of the snake
Lurking in the grass.

SECTION VI

This section is the last in this collection but it's dealing with a subject most men keep hidden. Love and women. All kinds of things run thru our minds. Why did we do her wrong? What could I have done different? I'm going to spoil her when I get home... Is she cheating on me? Why doesn't she stand by me like she use to? Is their somebody out there that is better for me? Men go thru a lot and the strongest ones either have a good woman or know that they have you finish that bid whether she'll be there or not. As for me well I've had my share of good, great, and less than desirable. So in this section you will see glimpses of what I wanted and what I had. The thing that sticks out the most in my mind is that I couldn't love or appreciate any woman until I loved and appreciated myself.

LOVE IS A ROSE

Love is like a rose
It begins as a seed.
Then as you nurture it with food and water
It grows.

As it grows it blossoms,
Now it's beautiful
And the aroma of that beauty precedes it.

A rose has thorns that will hurt and even draw blood
If they prick the skin.
This is no coincidence
It protects the beauty that lies
Within the rose.

If you neglect a rose
Or smother it
You can ruin it.

The petals will dry up
And fall off.
All that remains is the thorns
Mocking the beauty
That was once there.

I knew a love like that once.
It was beautiful
And the fumes from that love
Filled my nostrils.

We protected each other,
Maybe too much,
Maybe not enough.
Because the petals of that love
Withered away.

All that remains is the thorn
Of remembrance.
Lodged in my heart,
Drawing blood.

Love is a rose.

BEAUTY IS HER NAME

I lost faith in the world because of the things that I've had to endure.
Everything and everyone was ugly and dark.
Then I met her!

The sun began to shine brighter and the sea began to roar.
The grass was green and the flowers filled my nostrils with their
aroma.
Beauty is her name!

Casual conversation enriched my inner man.
Then it stimulated my outer shell, and I
Made love to her mind.

Only after that did I notice her physical beauty.
Her ivory white teeth, her golden brown hair.
Her complexion looked as if she was baked in the sun,
And the timer was set on golden brown.

Perfection was perfected in our union.
Individually we had our flaws but together we were unstoppable.
Certain individuals despised our union because of envy.

Nevertheless love conquers hate
And there is no distance that love can't overcome.
She taught me that, in spite of my dark heart.

Again, I say Beauty is her name.

SO SEDUCTIVE

Stepping into a room
Commanding attention
Without saying a word.
She's so seductive...

The way her eyebrows are arched,
Lip-gloss wets her lips, and her
Hair falls on her shoulders,
Yet, blows with the wind.
She's so seductive...

She doesn't walk,
She glides...her long
Shapely legs and graceful
Strides make the ground
Jealous that her bare feet aren't
Making direct contact with it.
Men are mesmerized, even
Women stop and stare.
She's so seductive...

Her outfit isn't overly covering
Or to revealing. It leaves
Just enough to the imagination
While simultaneously highlighting
The curvature of her breast and butt
While allowing a glimpse of her
Flat stomach.
She's so seductive...

She has an air of confidence
That comes with knowing that you
Are a force to be reckoned with,
But she's far from snobbish.
She's humble and independent
And is attracted by romance
Not finance.
Ooh…She's so seductive.

CAN YOU IMAGINE

Imagine if we were the last two people on earth.
Stranded on an exotic island
Feeding each other fresh fruit.

Can you imagine it?
Could you live a life like that...
With me?

Imagine if night fell and we're sitting under the stars
Re-affirming our commitment to one another
And a fire sparks out of the passion of our fantasies.

Can you imagine it?
Would you want to live a life like that...
With me?

Imagine if you awoke and all of that was a dream.
Then I appear and we're standing face to face,
We embrace and I whisper I love you.

Can you imagine it?
Do you want me to treat you like that
Forever?

Imagine if all you needs were met through me.
Imagine if I shared in your pleasure and comforted your pain.
Imagine if there was no need for secrets because
We lay naked and exposed to one another.

Can you imagine that?
I can!

A CONVERSATION WITH HER

I have so many questions for you
Hopefully you have some answers.

I must ask you this first...
Do you still love me?

Because I never stopped loving you,
Not out of necessity, it my choice!

I want to love you...
I want to romance you...
I want to share in your wildest dreams coming true...

How do we go from here?
One day at a time!

That day will turn to weeks, to months, to years.

I choose you...
To support...
To provide for...
To start a family with...

Yes, I still love you too!

IF

If only I had the opportunity
To whisper in your ear.
The secret I would reveal to you
Would make everything become crystal clear.

If only I had the opportunity
To hold you in my arms,
I'd gaze into your eyes
And set off your inner most alarms.

If only I had the opportunity
To rub my fingers in your hair.
I could confirm with my touch
That this is the end of your despair.

If is a mighty strong word
It adds emphasis to a wide variety of things.
Two letters stuck together
Attached to millions of people's dreams.

Imagine if we stuck that close together
Can you see how far we'd go?
The possibilities are endless
Yet only you and I will know
If...

STANDARDS

Excuse me lady, may I have
A quick conversation with you?

It seems every woman screams she has standards
Like it's something new.

Quite contrary most men
I know have standards too.

Yeah, we're after more
Than a big butt and a cute smile.

We consider a real woman one with
Both conversation and style.

Don't be deceived by the lust
That we seem to enjoy.

Because when commitment comes into play
You won't be our choice.

You seem to be impressed
With money and bling.

And let's not forget
The way the tree swings.

After one night stands
You wonder why men don't call.

Well, if he didn't drive a Benz
You wouldn't want to be bothered at all.

That's why

When we present the ring.

It's to the one
That makes our heart sing.

It didn't matter if we walked
Or rode the bus.

All that mattered was when
U and I formed us.
Her first question wasn't
Where are you employed?

She simply started talking
About the last book she enjoyed.

The focus wasn't on where we started
But where we were going.

And thru years of sacrifice
We'll make one hell of a sowing.

So, don't think that
All the good men are taken.

They're just waiting on a woman
Who is beyond all the faking?

Financial and physical dimensions
Fluctuate over time.

While intellectual and emotional qualities
Withstand the sands of time.

A TOUCH

It was a cloudy day in my life.
Everything that could go
Wrong did.

I told my lover
And she touched me.

My heart skipped a beat
Because my burdens were
Lifted. The clouds shifted,
The sun came out and
Smiled on me.

A slight pep was introduced
To my step. When I walked
I had a swagger about myself.

My confidence was boosted
And my countenance brightened
All because she touched me.

Words were not needed
Because of the energy transferred.

It said I love you no matter what.
Whether you're rich or poor I'm here.
To listen, to love, to support you!

Tears rimmed her eyes as she looked at me.
And my fingers wiped them away.

The water that poured from
The tears of her heart saturated
My fingers and watered my soul.

New growth was formed. A
New respect, admiration, and
A bond grew from the waters
Of her heart to the desert
Of my soul…
Thru a touch!

I WONDER

Looking out my window
At that chain linked barbed wire fence,
I noticed there isn't a single star in the sky.

Then I began to wonder,
Would my heart be that black
If I didn't let you inside.

THE GIFT AND THE CURSE

I was blessed with the ability to love
And cursed by being a man.
That's why I do the things I know aren't good for me.

At certain times in a mans life
Rational thinking escapes him.

Love is one of those times.
Love is a bully,
It is big and strong.

Strong enough to enter into a dark heart
And push anger and hate out.
It adds light to a darkened room.

Then manhood kicks in and says
"You're being soft, she has you whipped"
My reply is "Let love whip me and desire heal the wounds."

ILLUSIONS

Illusions of you and I
Together again.
Knowing deep down inside
The possibility of that is slim.

But in the depths of my heart…
I feel you…
I feel the love we once shared.

And in the recesses of my mind
I see us…
Together, smiling, and holding one another.

He gazing into your eyes
As you rub my back.
I take a deep breath
And capture a whiff
Of your scent.

Caught up in the rapture of us…
That is until reality knocks on
The door of my heart and looks
Into the window of my mind and
Tells me it's just an illusion.

DARE TO DREAM

Have you ever dared to dream
Of someone to endear?
As if you're looking in the mirror
The picture couldn't possibly become clearer.

Now if your dream became reality
Would you notice that?
If it stepped right out of your imagination
And some how landed in your lap.

If you ponder those two questions
It should be pain to see.
Why my speech starts to slur and heartbeat accelerates
When you get close to me.

You couldn't imagine how many sleepless nights
Were dedicated to thoughts of you.
Now that you are apart of my life
I realize there are some things I must cut loose.

Stepping out of childish ways
And putting on the shoes of a man.
My load has become a whole lot lighter
And it's because I found my dream and we're walking hand in hand.

WE BELONG TOGETHER

Dedicated to the past
And don't see a future in sight.
Lord show me a sign
Let me know if I'm right.

Holding broken dreams
Wondering if they will ever come true.
Emotion filled thoughts
Constantly surrounded by memories of you.

How did this happen?
Where did we go astray?
Lord I want my lady back
On this night I pray.

Looking in the stars
Reminds me of the twinkle in your eye.
We were a match made in heaven
To everyone surprise.

Doomed from the start
But a fighter in my spirit.
Crying inside
Yet no one seems to hear it.

There is an ache inside
Only to be soothed by you.
I believe we belong together
But you have to believe it too!

A DEEP LOVE

Have you ever-loved do deeply
That your feelings didn't matter?
Knowing that if you were ever separated from your lover
That your heart would simply shatter.

Envisioning your hands entangled with mine
While looking into your eyes with no concept of time.

As I look into your eyes
Do you know what I see?
Visions of happily ever after
A life shared between you and me.

This isn't hope nor is it a fantasy
It's a knowing in my soul
That burns to the core of me.

I often wonder what you're doing
And how your time is being spent.
Checking the catalog of my memories
To retrieve a whiff of your scent.

Recalling the feeling from a simple look into your eyes.
Thinking of ways to show my love,
Which is locked deep inside.

Entertaining thoughts of rubbing my fingers through your hair.
Massaging your shoulders, back, then feet
All after bathing you with care.

Trying to make you feel like the queen
That you are.
You give me the feeling of not only
Reaching but obtaining the stars!

I Love You

OBJECT OF MY AFFECTION II

Every man that I know
Holds a woman close to
His heart.

Whether he admits
It or not.

That doesn't make you soft
It actually makes you
More of a man,
Because you're not afraid to love.

In my case you are
And always will be
The object of my affection.

Thinking about days passed.
When you listened to me,
Consoled me, and gave me the
Advice that I needed.
Even when I didn't want
To heat it.

You've seen the mistakes
That I made.
You've seen me at my strongest
And my weakest.
You've seen my highs
And lows.

And you still loved me the same.

Regardless of,
In spite of,
Unapologetically
And Unconditionally.

You're not only my heart
You are the rhythm of
Its beat.

That's why your voice makes
My smile widen and your touch
Makes my knees weak.

I love you…
By choice!
I want you…
Forever!
You're the best thing for me and…
I know it!

That's why I Love You!

NOT YOUR...

I know it's hard for you to understand me.
Simply because you haven't been
Loved like this before.

But sweetheart I want to love you,
Not the outward part of you
That everyone sees.

Not your beautiful skin,
Not your perfect smile,
Not your sensuous touch,
Not you immaculate hands and feet.

Not even your firm breast
Or you're round buttock.
Not the money you make,
Not the car you drive,
Not the home you live in.

That's the easy part of you
To love...the part after
The dream came true.

Baby when I say
Let me love you
I'm saying let me love
You thru the process that
Led you to be what you
Are now.

I WANT TO

I want to know and love
Your pain. So I can better
Relate to your pleasure.

I want to love your insecurities
So I can appreciate your
Confidence.

I want to love you in the
Hard times when everyone
Else draws the line. So you'll
Know when I say I'm with you
I am.

I want to love you in
Sickness. So I can enjoy
Your health.

I want to love you when
You're penniless so that
You'll know that our love
Is priceless.

LET ME LOVE YOU

Let me love your flaws.
Let me love your doubts.
Let me love your insecurities.
Let me love your blemishes.
Let me love your imperfections.

Let me love you when you stumble.
Let me love you when you fall.
Let me love you when you don't love yourself.

Let me love the real you,
The you that's under the skin,
The you that no one else sees.

Let Me Love You